TABLE OF

MW01232339

Copyright

Introduction

About the Author

Mel Sillmon earned an MBA from the University of Dayton and was a Supply Chain Executive, with a successful career of over 30 years at Ford Motor Company. Mel also taught strategic management and organizational behavior at the University of Michigan, Dearborn, Michigan.

Mel developed the core competency and career model concept out of necessity and persistence and focused drive on moving up the corporate ladder.

Mel was told time and time again by many supervisors and managers at Ford of what experiences and competencies that he did not have to move up the corporate ladder.

Consequently, Mel set out to discover the essential skills and competencies that the top Fortune 500 companies recognized as critical to the progressive movement, up the Corporate Ladder.

Mel developed a strong core competency and career model process that had helped him to move from an entry pay grade level (5) Industrial Engineer to an executive pay grade level (14), Supply Chain Plant Group Manager, Ford.

Introduction

I taught an employee how to use the career mapping process. Over three weeks had passed, and I had not heard from the employee. So I called the fellow and asked, "why is it taking you so long to complete the career map process"? He stated Mel this was a robust process, and I do not like what the career map plan is suggesting that I pursue.

The map indicated that his competency strengths were in manufacturing and that he should pursue that career path and there were substantial gaps between his career goals and current skill level. Therefore, he realigned his goals and developed a realistic career map to obtain the required core competencies and was later successful in achieving his career goals.

Mel also used the career model process to identify transferable skills that helped him achieve an OR Supply Chain Manager position, in healthcare at the University of Michigan, Ann Arbor.

The critical elements of the career mapping process consist of defining your core competencies, mind mapping, gap analysis, and career strategic planning. I knew that I had discovered a valuable method, after meeting with a Group Vice President at Ford for only 15 minutes, and he stated, Mel please give me a copy of your process, it's fantastic.

Design Your Career with Passion

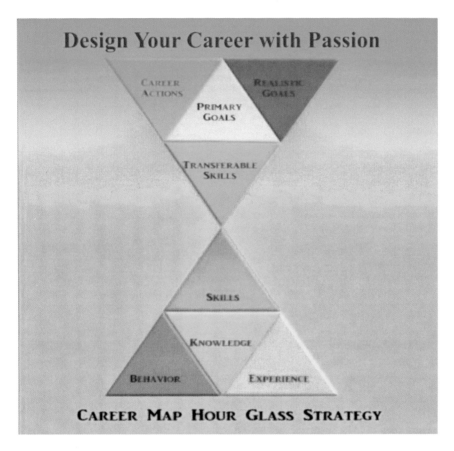

Your Career Success is driven primarily by the actions that you take now or don't take now. One should consider the implications of the "Career Map Hour Glass" in the development of your Career Map and or Strategy, on your future success.

When Designing Your Career

"Think not of yourself as the architect of your career but as the sculptor."

B. C. Forbes

Your Career is in your hands

"Your work is going to fill a large part of your life, and the only way to be truly satisfied is to do what you believe is great work. The only way to do great work is to love what you do." Steve Jobs

CREATING YOUR CAREER MAP

Career Mapping will help you:

- Identify your transferable skills, specialized knowledge, and experiences

- Discover realistic career opportunities that will match what you have to offer

- Learn how to move from career ideas to a concrete plan of action

Defining Your Core Competencies

How would you describe your accomplishments:

- Things that I have done?

- Things I can do?

- Things I will do?

Demonstrated competencies (accomplishments)

Core Competency Defined

Competency is defined as knowledge, skills, experiences and behaviors that your need to succeed in your role or career.

- Knowledge is what I know

- Skill is what I can do

- Behavior is how I act

- Experience is what I have done or

Define Your Passionate Career Path

Now please describe your ideal position in concept terms.
I want an analytical position, involves problem-solving, has a career path that.......

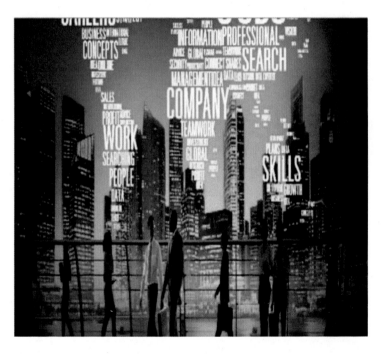

"Passion is the difference between having a job or having a career" www.behappy.me

CREATING YOUR CAREER MAP

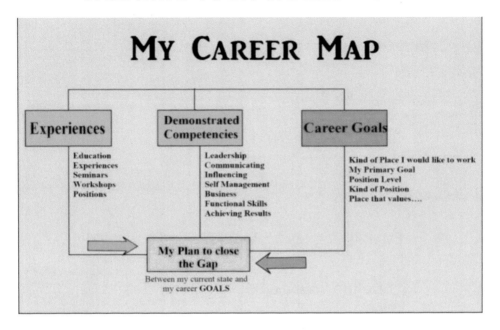

MY CAREER MAP

Experiences	Demonstrated Competencies	Career Goals
Education Experiences Seminars Workshops Positions	Leadership Communicating Influencing Self Management Business Functional Skills Achieving Results	Kind of Place I would like to work My Primary Goal Position Level Kind of Position Place that values....

My Plan to close the Gap

Between my current state and my career GOALS

Assess your functional and transferable Competencies, in terms of your style and what you like to do with:

- Things- Computers

- People- Collaboration

- Information- Analytics

People Competencies

Key Competencies that relates to people are:

- Leading others

- Communicating and Influencing

- Empowering others, confidence in others

- Establishing Focus, Listening and delegating

Define your people competencies

Reference: People Competencies, "The Value-Added Employee"

Core Competencies Root System

- The root system is the core competencies that nourish the core products (Careers).

- Construct your career map to demonstrate your mastery of skills required to achieve and prosper in a particular career.

- Focus on core competencies that will help you funnel individual skills and effort to achieve greater synergy and success.

- Define your core competencies roots.

Start with your passionate career (Goal) in mind.

Core Competencies Root System

Define your competencies roots:

Success

CAREER MAPPING PROCESS

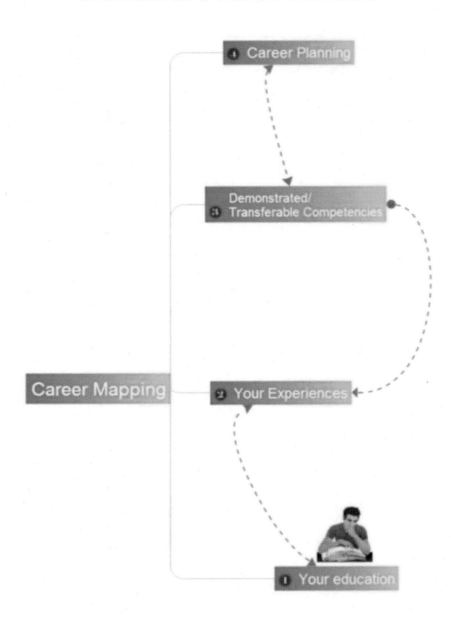

DEFINE YOUR EDUCATION

B.A.

M.B.A

Your education

Seminar/Workshops

Kaizen, Imai

Global Supply Chain Management, Kellogg Northwestern

Strategic Planning, University of Michigan

Lean, University of Michigan

Strategic Supply Chain, MIT

Seven Habits, Covey

Peak Performance, Davey

Peak Performance, A. Robbins

Six Sigma, Green Belt

Supply Chain Management, Graduate Class, Penn State

DEFINE YOUR EXPERIENCE

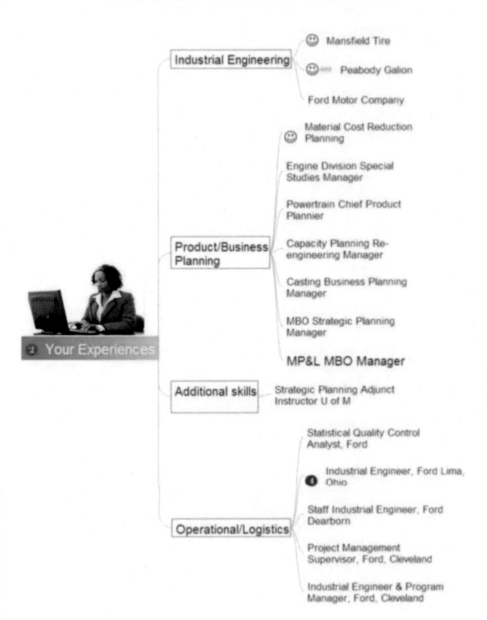

Your Experiences

- **Industrial Engineering**
  - Mansfield Tire
  - Peabody Galion
  - Ford Motor Company

- **Product/Business Planning**
  - Material Cost Reduction Planning
  - Engine Division Special Studies Manager
  - Powertrain Chief Product Plannier
  - Capacity Planning Re-engineering Manager
  - Casting Business Planning Manager
  - MBO Strategic Planning Manager
  - **MP&L MBO Manager**

- **Additional skills**
  - Strategic Planning Adjunct Instructor U of M

- **Operational/Logistics**
  - Statistical Quality Control Analyst, Ford
  - Industrial Engineer, Ford Lima, Ohio
  - Staff Industrial Engineer, Ford Dearborn
  - Project Management Supervisor, Ford, Cleveland
  - Industrial Engineer & Program Manager, Ford, Cleveland

DEFINE YOUR COMPETENCIES

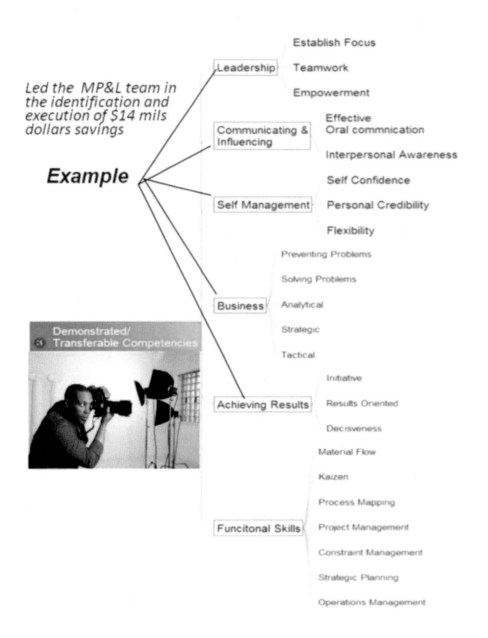

Led the MP&L team in the identification and execution of $14 mils dollars savings

Example

Leadership
- Establish Focus
- Teamwork
- Empowerment

Communicating & Influencing
- Effective Oral commnication
- Interpersonal Awareness

Self Management
- Self Confidence
- Personal Credibility
- Flexibility

Business
- Preventing Problems
- Solving Problems
- Analytical
- Strategic
- Tactical

Achieving Results
- Initiative
- Results Oriented
- Decisveness

Funcitonal Skills
- Material Flow
- Kaizen
- Process Mapping
- Project Management
- Constraint Management
- Strategic Planning
- Operations Management

Demonstrated/ Transferable Competencies

DEFINE YOUR CAREER GOALS, GAPS AND ROADMAP

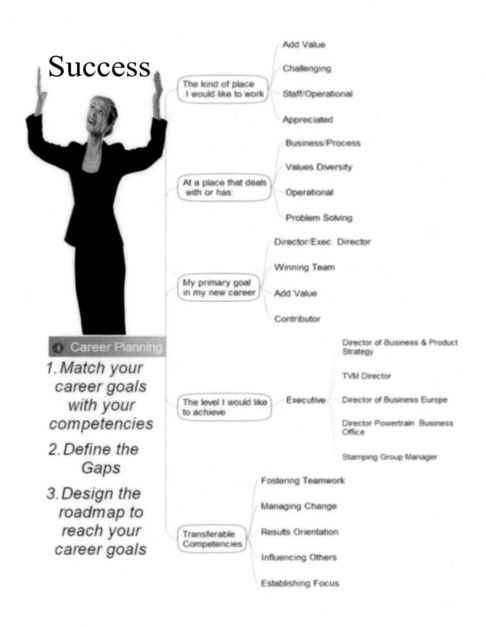

Success

Career Planning

1. Match your career goals with your competencies

2. Define the Gaps

3. Design the roadmap to reach your career goals

The kind of place I would like to work
- Add Value
- Challenging
- Staff/Operational
- Appreciated

At a place that deals with or has:
- Business/Process
- Values Diversity
- Operational
- Problem Solving

My primary goal in my new career
- Director/Exec. Director
- Winning Team
- Add Value
- Contributor

The level I would like to achieve — Executive
- Director of Business & Product Strategy
- TVM Director
- Director of Business Europe
- Director Powertrain Business Office
- Stamping Group Manager

Transferable Competencies
- Fostering Teamwork
- Managing Change
- Results Orientation
- Influencing Others
- Establishing Focus

Teamwork

Teamwork, compelling dialogue and critical conversation competencies are crucial to your effectiveness in business today.

CLOSING THOUGHTS

Remember that you are the Sculptor of your career

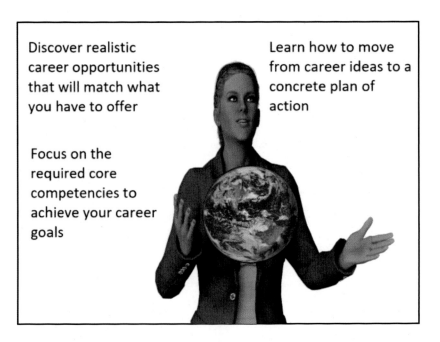

Discover realistic career opportunities that will match what you have to offer

Learn how to move from career ideas to a concrete plan of action

Focus on the required core competencies to achieve your career goals

Visualize yourself as being successful!

References:

Mind mapping, Joyce Wycoff, 1991

A Fork In the Road, Susan Maltz and Barbara Grahn, 2003

The Value-Added Employee, Edward J. Cripe, Richard S. Mansfield, 2002

Notes

Notes

Made in the USA
Monee, IL
20 September 2022

14341195R00017